Patience

Patience

Leadership-Competence-Motivation-Success

Progressive Youth Series

Virender Kapoor

PATIENCE
Virender Kapoor

Published by Qurate Books Pvt. Ltd.

© Virender Kapoor

Published in 2023

ISBN: 978-81-96261-80-1

Qurate Books Pvt. Ltd.
Goa 403523, India
www.quratebooks.com
Tel: 1800-210-6527, Email: info@quratebooks.com

Table of Contents

Introduction   vii

1   The Philosophy of Patience   1
2   You Can't Change The Fundamentals—
    Wishes are not Always Granted   6
3   Yes, You Can: Patience is a Decision you can Take   8
4   Change is The Only Constant   13
5   Numbers can Crush Us—Stop Counting   17
6   Prioritize your Requirements   23
7   Being in The Moment   30
8   How to use Social Media and the Mobile Phone
    to Build Patience   35
9   On Doing Nothing   42
10 Handling Rage   48
11 Some Exercises   52
12 Love Yourself   57

Self-Assessment Questions—Patience Shortgasm   59

Introduction

TODAY, WE LIVE in an age of "hurry" or the "right now age"—RINA. It's all about, "I want this and I want it now and I want it the maximum and the best. " Quality, quantity, and hurry are the worst combination that makes us a constant cribber—the never happy types.

You have picked up this book with a purpose—to get into the habit of being patient.

People used to live a great life Forty years ago when they had plenty of time—enough leisure time. They would sit on a bench or even a huge log and chat away without any agenda—cracking jokes, gossiping, and talking aimlessly.

Today we have become more aimless, but we are in a hurry. We don't enjoy ourselves anymore because we are in a hurry—in a hurry to open the message, to react and respond, and to forward too. In the bargain, we have lost the ability to wait.

We set ourselves too many targets unnecessarily. CEOs are put on the edge every quarter as they need to declare profits and results. Earlier, we had five-year plans by the government; today we have hundred-day report cards of the government too! We make each other's life hell for no good reason. We create unnecessary targets. I call these "self-inflicted injuries." In every activity, you to take an oath *"Main jo bhi karoonga, jaldi karoonga. Jaldi ke siwa ye kuch nahi karoonga!"* (Whatever I do, I will do it in a hurry and will do nothing without hurry!) This is a perfect recipe for disaster.

Earlier, we just had time. Today we have real time, quality time, me time, happy time (in a restaurant), but actually we have no time. We have become impatient, and that is affecting our happiness and health.

In simple words, "patience" means the ability to wait calmly in the face of distress, disappointment, and suffering. To wait for your turn. Most important is when you look at patience on the time axis. Waiting in a queue—it's taking too long; waiting in a traffic jam—it's taking too long; waiting for an announcement—it's taking too long . So generally we look at patience within the time continuum. The other way of not remaining calm, cool, composed, and unruffled is dealing with some awkward guy, a bad friend, a dumb guy who just don't understand, a child making the same mistake again and again, or teaching your younger brother something and he just doesn't understand, or a baby who doesn't stop crying, or a fly that keeps coming and sitting on your nose, or a mosquito coming again and again buzzing in your ear.

Actually it is combination of both—time and emotional response, (measured or volcanic).

You can wait patiently listening to some nonsense from your friend for ten minutes, who is continuously yelling and narrating an incident that doesn't concern you, and you keep standing there (waiting for him to finish) —that is time. And once he has finished, you don't catch him by the throat or hit him; you just stand like a cool guy, not reacting to the incident at all (emotional control). Therefore, patience is with respect to time as well as control of your emotions.

The other two angles regarding patience are being fidgety or worrying about the outcome or consequences. Let me explain. You have a choice of songs on YouTube or a collection on your gadget and you can't stick to one singer; you first go to the best of Kishore Kumar, then in a minute you switch to Mohammad Rafi, then quickly to Sonu Nigam, and then to Mika Singh! You are fidgety and can't stick to something even for a minute. Or on FM radio, you keep changing radio stations recklessly. Earlier, we had limited choices; we were served what the Hindi or English songs that were available. We expected something good every time and enjoyed what came our way. So to keep shifting between choices is a kind of impatience.

Another nuance of patience is not being able to wait for the result. Let's say you appeared in a competitive exam and the result has to be uploaded on the website next morning. Your concern is, "Did I make it or not?" You can be patient or impatient while waiting. Your impatience is not going to change the result. The consequences of the result weigh heavy on your mind. Your life can hang by a thread or you can be cool and take it as it comes. Here too, emotions play up. Therefore, at the heart of patience is the control of emotions and self-control. We will discuss all these aspects in the book and try to find solutions.

This is the most important quality for our success and more importantly your health and happiness—CHILL. Patience is nothing but to chill in any situation. Simple? No. It looks like it is, but it is not. NOT AT ALL. That is why this book—it is Wisdom just to teach you to CHILL—to take a chill pill.

Virender Kapoor

1
The Philosophy of Patience

I have seen many storms in my life. Most storms have caught me by surprise, so I had to learn very quickly to look further and understand that I am not capable of controlling the weather, to exercise the art of patience and to respect the fury of nature.

—Paulo Coelho

PATIENCE HAS SEVERAL connotations that must be understood to appreciate its impact on human beings. We then need to look at ways and means to adapt them in our life.

The Philosophy of Patience
Patience means to be able to endure—endure mentally. Some people think that such endurance and forbearance is cowardice and a sign of weakness—a tendency to give up.

But this is a misnomer. Patience is the greatest power. All religions promote the thought that God provides support to those who live in this world with patience. Ancient books like the Bhagavad Gita have recognized the importance of patience through quotes like: "Little by little, through patience and repeated effort, the mind will become stilled in the Self." If we examine our self as a part of nature, we will realize that even nature creates change very slowly and is extremely patient.

This is no religious philosophy; rather, it is based on the law of nature. You plant a seed and keep watering it for weeks together, and only then a tree starts growing. Patience is different from waiting. Instead, we have to do the work first, lay the foundation, plant the seed, make sure the soil is right or prepared, get ready, and then wait for all the elements to fall into place before making the right decision that will drive us to greater success.

There are many examples that illustrate how patience has helped people achieve success. Isaac Newton, the father of modern science, would often remain silent when he was young, which gave him the epithet "woolgatherer." Later, it was discovered that Newton had the extraordinary ability to concentrate on a point. This could have not happened without patience.

The most important advantage of having patience is that it helps us in handling frustration without really getting frustrated. It also protects our well-being in stressful situations and keeps our mind, body, and- soul in balance. People who are patient have better interpersonal relationships. Patience directly and positively impacts mental and hence physical health of an individual. Studies point out that patient people suffer less depression and experience a much happier life. They live life better than those who are impatient. It has been found that there is a positive relationship between patience, optimism, and hope.

Patience is contentment and contentment brings patience. If you are always longing for more, you will always be restless and impatient. Patience not only requires courage but contentment. Much of our impatience in life is a result of discontentment with friends, with ourselves, and with the way things are going in general.

Patience makes us more resilient, more tolerant, and ultimately, more efficient. A patient person conserves his energy and breath for action time and doesn't waste body fuel just by revving up at one place on a motor bike.

Patience is kindness. When someone weaker than you irritates you or expects something from you, your behavior reflects your character. If you yell at a beggar if he constantly nags you to give him some money, you have lost the plot. If a waiter by mistake trips on something and spills water over you and you lose your cool, again you have lost the plot. Therefore, once you demonstrate restraint in the most trying or irritating situations, you have demonstrated strong character and great self-control. Often times, the right thing or the kind thing is not the easiest thing, but it is always worth doing anyway.

Patience is most important for seekers. Meditation and concentration are important for seekers—seekers of God and seekers of truth. It requires a lot of patience to come even anywhere near enlightenment. Do you thing Lord Buddha got his final wisdom and enlightenment in a jiffy? No, it took him years of meditation.

When you pray to God for something, your prayers are not answered immediately. You need to be patient with God too. He does not have all the time for you; your time will come—the time decided by the Lord. God's time is not always your time. Unfortunately, today, you want an instant God too! People go to Shirdi Sai Baba and look for shortcuts to "Baba's Darshan." But you will get *darshan* only when he decides. Your car may break down on the way; he may be checking your dedication by putting obstacles along your journey, which may get delayed by several hours. People ask for shorter and more potent *pujas* at home. The *panditji* or priest is bribed to take shortcuts so that you can do a quickie puja!

When you are sick, prayer gives you strength to wait patiently so that you can recover slowly but surely. If you wait patiently, you will show mercy to yourself. Crying and cribbing all the time will not cure you faster. It will take its own time.

Let Things Settle Down

"Let things cool down," and "let the dust settle down" are common expressions. Actually, they are nothing but different expressions to convey patience.

Lord Buddha once was traveling with his disciples across vast distance from one town to another. They halted to take rest near a small rivulet. Buddha asked one of the youngest to go get him some water to drink. As the young boy approached the water body, he saw two cows crossing the river, and due to that, water became muddy and unfit for drinking. He returned to Buddha and told him that the water was muddy as cows had just crossed the water body. Buddha waited for an hour and asked him to go again, but he again came back and said that the water was muddy. After another half hour, Buddha asked him to go again. Though a little irritated, the young man went again and found that the water was absolutely crystal clear and he filled a pitcher and brought it to Buddha. Buddha asked, "What did you do to clean the water?" He said, "I did nothing. The mud settled down by itself with time." This was a practical way of teaching patience.

Therefore, give time for the chaos around you or a bad situation to settle down.

The Connection Between Compassion, Forgiveness, and Patience

When you hold a grudge or hate someone, you are keeping pent-up anger, a sort of poison, within you, which keeps troubling you as long as it remains within your mind and heart. It releases only once you forgive the person who wronged you. Therefore, the compassion you show for someone actually is compassion for you. By showing compassion for someone, you are showing compassion towards yourself.

It is like freeing your soul. Similarly, when you are impatient, you are harming yourself—that is the fact of the matter. There is therefore a direct connect between compassion and patience? When you are patient, you are compassionate to yourself.

Have patience with all things but first with yourself.

—Saint Francis de Sales

2

You Can't Change The Fundamentals—Wishes are not Always Granted

If wishes were horses, beggars would ride.

—Scottish proverb

REMEMBER, THE WORLD does not move according to you; instead, you need to move according to the world. This is at the heart and core of patience. You always wish that things happen as per your desire, so you say, "I wish such and such a thing would happen," but it does not happen, and you get disappointed. This wish list can be never-ending. "I wish my friend would understands me," "I wish my teacher gives me extra days to submit the assignment," "I wish I get better marks without studying much," "I wish I get first rank in the class," "I wish my parents would understand my problems," and this list gets longer and longer. You end up accumulating a lot of pressure within you, which keeps increasing as things don't go according to your wishes.

If you clip/shorten your wish list, you will be happier. Instant or *tatkal* wishing is very dangerous and distressing, the mentality of "I want something and I want it right now."

This is related to the time function. You reach a restaurant and you see a huge crowd waiting to get in and there is a waiting list. You think, "Oh my God! I can't wait. I wish the people sitting inside the restaurant eat a little faster! OMG, can you even imagine this can happen?"

The height of wishing is a quote by George Carlin: "May the forces of evil become confused on the way to your house."

You wish that the train comes on time so that you don't have to wait on the platform. You hope people move faster in the queue for the cinema tickets, but that does not happen. Well, reduce your wish list and your expectations, and you will be happy. There is an old saying, "The contented one is who is happy with his portion." Learn to be happy with what you have. The grass always looks greener on the other side.

At the same time, people tell us to always think big, aim high, and make loftier dreams. That is good as long as your aims are realistic, achievable, and practical.

You want to be rich and you want It right now. Now the first part of the wish is fine but the second part isn't.

The fundamentals can't be changed; they are according to the nature. If it takes half an hour to bake a cake, it takes half an hour. By increasing the temperature of the oven, you will only burn the cake but not get it any faster. If sunrise is at 6:00 a.m., you can do nothing to change it, so synchronize your routine according to the sunrise and don't say wish for sunrise at 7:00 a.m. Because that is not going to happen. Here is a wonderful quote that summarizes and captures the essence of what I am saying in this chapter:

> God, grant me the serenity to accept the things I cannot change, the courage to change the things I can, and the wisdom to know the difference."
>
> —Reinhold Niebuhr

3

Yes, You Can: Patience is a Decision you can Take

Patience is a virtue, and I'm learning patience.
It's a tough lesson.

—Elon Musk

THE ABOVE QUOTE sounds simple because it is simple. The human mind has so much strength that one doesn't really understand how strong it is. Once you decide on something, you will be surprised at how effectively you can hold on to your decision. Great as well as not-so-great people have shown how the power of decision works for them.

A prison sentence can be very painful. You are isolated, put in uncomfortable accommodation, and you are a convict by title. You have no name, you have a number.

Nelson Mandela: A Great Example of patience
Nelson Mandela was imprisoned for twenty-seven long years. Try to imagine how long twenty-seven years is. Life imprisonment in our

country is fourteen years, but this was an unconditional, unlimited jail sentence. He was just a number—prisoner number 46664. He had resilience and he had a sense of humor and the ability to laugh at himself, and probably these helped him wait out the twenty-seven years patiently.

He said, "I went for a long holiday for twenty-seven years," referring to his years in prison. This is an attitude, and a patient attitude helps you survive such an ordeal.

He was a member of the African National Congress (ANC), which was fighting against apartheid. He was arrested and imprisoned in 1962, and subsequently sentenced to life imprisonment for conspiring to overthrow the state. Mandela's twenty-seven years in prison were split between Robben Island, Pollsmoor Prison, and Victor Verster Prison.

The notorious Robben Island, close to the city of Cape Town, acquired its name from the seals that once populated it; a seal is called *robben* in Dutch. Its three centuries as a prison island and a place of banishment were punctuated by a period as a leper colony.

A prison warden greeted him saying, "This is the Island. This is where you will die." What a way to greet someone—it can be shattering for a person. A prison sentence of three years or seven years gives you hope that one day you will be free, but this was an unconditional, hopeless situation—life imprisonment till death.

They were housed in a new cell block constructed for political prisoners. The wardens were rude and tough on them. Each had a single cell with a slop bucket, some seven foot square, around a concrete courtyard. To start with, they were allowed no reading material. It was difficult to kill time, and that is what a cell does to you.

They crushed stones with a hammer to make gravel and were made to work in a blindingly bright quarry, digging out limestone. They had been sentenced to rigorous imprisonment (RI).

Nelson Mandela frequently criticized the prison staff for ill-treating them and was very often taught a lesson by being locked in isolation. This was the worst mental torture as passing time in isolation is not easy and one can go crazy in such a situation. Staying calm and patient was the only way to survive.

"In those early years, isolation became a habit. We were routinely charged for the smallest infractions and sentenced to isolation," he wrote in his autobiography, *The Long Walk to Freedom*. "The authorities believed that isolation was the cure for our defiance and rebelliousness. I found solitary confinement the most forbidding aspect of prison life. There was no end and no beginning; there is only one's own mind, which can begin to play tricks."

Prison authorities normally create unpleasant conditions for prisoners to teach them a lesson. These were political prisoners, and they could not expect any mercy from the wardens.

Even in jails for criminals or under trials, unfortunately, very little mercy is shown to prisoners. In India, jails are often overcrowded with poor hygiene conditions. Wardens can be heartless. Mandela chose to be patient so that his misery would be less burdensome.

Meditation can be good for jail staff as well as the inmates. Dr. Kiran Bedi, a lady Indian Police Service (IPS) officer who was posted as inspector general (IG) of prisons at Tihar Jail (most notorious for being harsh on prisoners), wanted to change whatever she could. She started a Vipassana (meditation) course for staff and inmates, and it did them a lot good. Vipassana is a natural way to calm your mind and also develop patience.

Nelson Mandela was no ordinary prisoner. He was destined to become the first black president of the country. He described that prison can be mentally challenging because of the mundane routine. You have no freedom of choice. "Each day like the one before; each week like the one before it, so that the months and years blend into each other," Mandela wrote in his book.

Books can be great partners and a great way to pass time constructively. Initially, they were not allowed any reading material, but when the prisoners, led by Mandela, insisted and persisted, they were given reading material. Although some subjects such as politics and military history were forbidden, Robben Island became known as a "university behind bars." To make matters worse, he was not allowed to attend the funeral of his son who died in an accident. But he endured . . . endured patiently.

The Tale of a Taxi Driver

For one cab driver, his decision to take a moment to slow down for one woman changed everything. This is a story of patience and brotherhood . . . of mankind. It's a story of small, random acts of kindness that have the power to affect people on a big scale.

The taxi driver arrived at the address and honked the horn. After waiting a few minutes, he honked again. He parked his cab in the parking lot and walked up to the door and knocked for the passenger to show up. "Just a minute," answered a frail, elderly voice. After a long pause, the door opened. A small woman in her nineties stood before him. She was wearing a print dress and a pillbox hat with a veil pinned on it. By her side was a tiny suitcase. The apartment looked dilapidated, as if no one had lived in it for years.

"Would you please carry this suitcase to the car?" she said. He reluctantly took the suitcase to the cab and then returned to assist the old lady. He felt sorry for her as she was all alone.

She took his arm, and they walked slowly towards the parking lot.

As she sat in the car, she said, "Oh, my God, you're such a good boy." She gave him the address and then asked, "Could you drive through downtown?"

"It's not the shortest way," he informed her, as a longer route would cost more.

"Oh, I don't mind," she said. "I'm in no hurry. I'm on my way to a hospital."

Her eyes were glistening, and he could see tiny teardrops on the sides of her eyes. "I don't have any family left," she continued in a soft voice. "The doctor says I don't have very long." He was so moved that he quietly reached over and shut off the meter.

"What route would you like me to take?" he asked. Though he himself was getting late to return home and be with his family, he chose not to hurry.

He chose to be kind and patient with someone who needed him badly. Someone who was helpless required his help, and he took a call to help the old, helpless lady.

On such occasions, one needs to take a call and decide to show kindness and be a little patient with the elderly.

Some people are cool and some are not, yet it is possible for everyone to choose to become cool and patient. It is ultimately your decision that matters.

If you are the impatient type, you need to take this decision again and again, you have to remind yourself again and again till you make it a habit. Remember, bad habits are difficult to shed but not impossible to get rid of.

You can try doing this with your nasty friend, a stupid neighbor, or a cranky sibling. Practice makes you perfect.

> Trust your instincts, and make judgements on what your heart tells you. The heart will not betray you.
>
> —David Gemmell, *Fall of Kings*

4

Change is The Only Constant

*Change is the law of the universe. You can be a million-
aire or a pauper in an instant.*

—*Bhagavad Gita*

THERE IS A beautiful Hindi song written by Gulzar and sung by the late Kishore Kumar, which says, *"Aney wala pall, Janewala hai, ho sake to isme zindagi bita do, pall joye janewala hai . . ."* (The moment that is to come will also go away, therefore if possible, spend your entire life in that moment because that moment is definitely going to go . . .)

This reveals the actual meaning of life—life is like a flowing river in which nothing stays. All things will pass away with time, nothing stays with you forever. Our life itself is not permanent. Stars, planets, and galaxies themselves are transient. They are created and then destroyed by nature. Trees don't live forever; they grow, flourish, and maybe in a few years, just die away.

Except for troubles, we want everything to be permanently with us!

Fortunately, both good things and bad things are never permanent. We want the pain in the back to disappear right now but the fragrance of an expensive perfume to stay on forever. Both are not possible. Both are transient, both will go away with time. We are okay with good things but are never fine with anything bad. How selfish and mean of us!

The great Charlie Chaplin had said, "Nothing is permanent in this world—not even your troubles."

The problem with us is that we want everything permanent in this life, which itself is not permanent; we forget that, in fact, nothing is in our control. We always want everything to be permanent—permanent happiness, permanent wealth, fortune, life, good health, and the list goes on. We live our life with plenty of delusions. We are like passengers. Someone gets into a train from one station and someone gets down at another.

I remember when I was young, I had gone with my parents to the funeral of some relative who was very rich. The wife of the deceased said, "*Sau saal ka saaman ikaththa kiya par kal ka pata nahi*" (we accumulate stuff for a hundred years—property, gold, and, say, cash—but we do not know what will happen tomorrow).

The Story of a King and a Saint

In this insightful story, a spiritual teacher came to the front door of the king's palace and managed to reach where the king was relaxing on a couch.

"What do you want?" asked the king, immediately recognizing the visitor.

"I would like a place to sleep in this inn of yours," replied the saint.

"But this is not an inn. It is my palace," said the king.

"May I ask who owned this palace before you?"

"My father owned it earlier. But he is dead."

"And who owned it before him?" asked the teacher.

"My grandfather owned it before that. He too is dead."

"And this place where people live for a short time and then move on—did I hear you say that it is not an inn?"

The king learnt his lesson and thanked the teacher for teaching him that he too would go one day. The whole world is in transition, in fact, the whole universe is constantly changing and so are we. From a toddler you have become a little boy, now you are a teen, then you become an adult, and then a mature, middle-aged person, and so on.

We tend to feel that all the troubles in the world are made for us only. In present times, people are so sensitive and emotional that small problems make them so stressed that want to end their own life. We have become so cowardly. We should not forget that life is a great gift of God, and we should never waste that gift by ending our life in that way.

We should always remember that all the trouble, all the problems have come to make us strong and that they will not stay for a long period of time. They will pass.

Therefore, never jump with joy if something great happens and never feel down in the dumps if something goes wrong. This is the best way to maintain balance of mind.

The Three-Year Test to Save You from Agony
The best way to handle a bad situation is to understand that the problem that is troubling you immensely right now may not trouble you after some time. That is why it is said, "Time is the greatest healer." So let it pass, and it will pass.

Let us say you missed your friend's birthday party. You feel that the world has come to an end as far as you are concerned. You are fretting and fuming the whole day, maybe for next few days. Or you lose a comic you bought last month. You scream, "Why the hell was I not careful?" and because of that, you can't think straight the whole day and annoy your parents and your friends. You are so upset that you forget to do your school assignment too.

In such a terrible situation, I suggest you take a piece of paper and write down the problem.

In this case you lost your favorite comic. Okay, what will the significance of this be after three years? You will see that you will laugh at yourself because this incident will be behind you in a week's time. That is why they say, "Don't cry over the spilt milk."

"Jo ho gaya, so ho gaya"—whatever has happened has happened. Get it out of your system—forgive yourself and move on.

> As we know, forgiveness of oneself is the hardest of all the forgiveness.
>
> —Joan Baez

Another solution for getting energy to face negative situation is to believe that God is with you always and that he will surely rescue you from all the adverse situations—this will give you mental strength to face all the troubles of this world.

> Mistakes are always forgivable, if one has the courage to admit them.
>
> —Bruce Lee

Life Itself Is a Compromise—It's a Part of Life

Remember, it is better to compromise on things you cannot change than keep sulking and augmenting the damage. "You may either win your peace or buy it: win it, by resistance to evil; buy it, by compromise with evil."

> I shall argue that strong men, conversely, know when to compromise and that all principles can be compromised to serve a greater principle.
>
> —Dale Carnegie

5

Numbers can Crush Us—Stop Counting

Not everything that counts can be counted and not everything that can be counted counts.

—Albert Einstein

Stop Counting and Start Living

Yes, numbers actually mess up our happiness. And many times, they just don't matter. However, we are obsessed with numbers and sizes.

I too have a bad habit of counting everything, and as I write this chapter, I realize I have to let go of these numbers.

Let's see. How many features do you have on your phone? Does it matter? You may have the latest phone upgraded with 131 features, for which you paid a bomb. But you may use not more than five out of the 131! Take a reality check. Your neighbor's car is fourteen inches longer than yours. How does it matter? He may have a problem parking it and would have paid five lakh rupees more than your dad did for his car. And you are impatient to get that car! Aren't you being stupid?

I bought the latest Mercedes Benz, and it took two weeks for me to get past half the features it came with. I don't even use most of them.

Whether one has five hundred crores or five crores in the bank, you live as well as the other. You can live very well anyways, so why worry? Car advertisements say, "This car runs from 0 to 100 km/hour in six seconds!" Must you drive that fast? Why are you in such a hurry? In fact, you would never require that kind of acceleration except if a cheetah starts chasing you! Stop counting and start living.

Sample this statement:

Today I am twenty-one years, ten months and seven days, and have spent 38 percent of that time complaining about how tired I am. I have tweeted 566 times and got twenty-seven likes and have more than thousand five hundred followers on my Twitter account. I have 4,567 friends on my Facebook account. I have more than 1,256 numbers in my phone directory and have twenty-four very good friends at school and a motorbike with a 500cc engine. I feel I have wasted three years three months and twenty days doing nothing.

Who the hell is interested in these numbers? Are you? I don't think so. We are so possessed by and obsessed with these numbers—from bank balance to credit card limits, to the number of cards you have to the number of friends on Facebook, to the floor area of your home to the size of the garden and the number of neighbors you know, the number of people who attended your birthday and the number of gifts you got, and this list never ends! We are only counting, counting, and counting. We ignore quality as long as we have the numbers (quantity).

And we suffer sleepless nights for these. We are ***impatient to have*** more friends on Twitter and Instagram, more friends around us, higher marks in every subject, more friends at school, more comics at home . . .

I remember when we first started using digital transmission, we had Nokia modems with a speed of 2400 bits per second, and as compared to the old telex system and teleprinters of 50 bits per second, it was a quantum leap! 50:2400 was a 48-time jump in speed. Today we have megabits per second and terabits per second systems, and we still want more. Because, we want everything faster and faster, clearer and clearer, bigger and bigger, smarter and smarter, more and more.

We are suffering from a *"dil maange more"* (I want more) syndrome. This is an impatience syndrome. We have created this situation for ourselves.

Pizza in thirty minutes or you don't pay. Hey, why not twenty-five minutes? Then why not fifteen minutes. Or right now, this minute. Instant coffee, two-minute noodles, heat and eat, ready to eat are the expressions . . . these reflect that marketing strategists are playing on your impatient psyche. Lose weight in two weeks, pay more and lose it in five days. Learn to speak fluent English or Spanish in thirty days, graduate in two years instead of three! Buy one, get two free.

We do not want to count; we want to think the count.

—Alain Badiou

Marketing Madness is Actually Public Madness
Most fitness gurus tell you that you must walk 10,000 steps a day—yes, a whopping ten thousand. Yes, the figure looks good—TEN K. But do you know why 10,000? Hold your heart.

This was started by a Japanese company called Yamasa Clock. The device was called Mapo-Kei, which in Japanese means "10,000 steps meter." This was a smart marketing gimmick. No one questioned it, and all the gurus and experts started saying that this was the best target! Can you believe this? If this is not herd mentality, then what is?

Latest research by Harvard Medical School has shown that 4,400 steps a day is pretty good and doing more than 7,500 steps a day has no benefit at all. The top-of-the-line target could be 7,500 and good enough could be mere 4,400 steps. If you walk 10,000 steps a day, even if you walk four days a week, it comes to 208 days in a year, which multiplied by 2,500 steps extra daily means 5,20,000 extra wasted steps in a year. Therefore, think before you fix targets.

We Get Fixated on Fixations

We ourselves make our lives miserable by fixing targets. How we reach these figures is not funny.

I am 80 kg today, and I must become 65 kg in next three months. That is losing 5 kg a month. How did this target come about? And worse, to lose it in three months. For heaven's sake, from where? Why not 10 kg and in four months? This is a fixated obsession, which if not achieved, frustrates you and irritates you, and in order to meet this you are restless, and in another words, impatient. It is a self-inflicted injury.

I should have 1,50,000 followers on Instagram. I should have one million visitors on my website and 20,000 e-mail subscribers. I must create a ten-million-dollar company evaluation in the next three years. Who says so, and why?

One cannot just ignore numbers because numbers give an idea of quantification. I am by no stretch of imagination suggesting that you ignore numbers all together. But be realistic; don't just fix numbers that are not rational or practical.

I start playing golf, and I want to become a zero handicap in one year. This is unrealistic. You will make your life miserable on the golf course with these kinds of fixations. So stop chasing and start living. Stop counting the score. Play the damn game and enjoy it in the literal sense of it. Life is a game; play it and enjoy it. Don't destroy your happiness along the way.

> I can calculate everything but not the number of moments in a second.
>
> —Khalid Masood

Numbers May Not Matter

Baking fish and a tourist: There was a man sitting under a tree on the beach baking two pomfret fish. A rich American man wearing a Rolex watch passed by and asked him, "Why did you catch only two fish from this big sea?"

The man said, "What else should I do?"

The rich man said, "Take a boat and go deep in and get a thousand fish."

The man said, "What do I do with so many fish?"

The American man replied, "Sell 998 and eat two."

"Then what?"

"Buy a bigger boat and get tons of fish and sell it and make $5000 more money."

"What then?" asked the man as he baked his fish.

"Buy a fleet of trawlers and make $10,000 a day," said the rich man.

"What do I do with 10,000 dollars a day?"

"You can do whatever you like to do. By the way, what do you like doing the most?" asked the rich man

"I like baking two fish on the beach every day," said the man, busy baking his two fish.

The man with the expensive watch fell silent.

If you are happy with two fish, why do you want tons of it? Your targets should be need-based not greed-based.

The moral of the story is that do what is actually required and not as per targets fixed by others. Do as much as is really required.

Have you seen people during weddings where there is a lavish spread of food? People fill up their plates to the brim as if there is no tomorrow. Then they can't finish it and throw it away in the garbage bin. What is this—need or greed? It definitely is greed. Never do this; you can always take a second helping.

Magic is a sudden opening of the mind to the wonder of existence. It is a sense that there is much more to life than we usually recognize; that we do not have to be confined by the limited views that our family, our society, or our own habitual thoughts impose on us; that life contains many dimensions, depths, textures, and meanings extending far beyond our familiar beliefs and concepts.

—John Welwood

6
Prioritize your Requirements

**Slow Down a Bit—Imagine Life is a Line and
You are Walking on it**

There is more to life than increasing its speed.

—Mahatma Gandhi

You Get Only One Life

Life is like a line on which you are walking from start to finish. If you run too fast, you will finish earlier; if you work/walk slowly, steadily, and happily, you will live longer.

We get impatient if a job is not done, especially jobs we are responsible to accomplish at home or at school. So live it well and you won't have any regrets once you have reached the end of the line. That is your life line.

We lose patience and get exasperated once we feel overwhelmed by the work that we have on the table. The major reason for this is that most—yes, most of us—are not organized.

The reason for this is we do not keep track of priorities. You may have a dozen jobs to do in a day; some are important, some are urgent, and some are least important. This is not cosmic science (it is a shade more complex than rocket science). This is common sense.

Multitasking is a myth. You cannot do parallel processing like a computer. Your brain is a human brain and is designed to handle one thing at a time while a computer is a computer and not your brain.

When we talk of multitasking, we mean that one can perform lots of things but not at the same time. There is a common perception that women are better at multitasking. It means a mother can cook, she can bathe a child, supervise arrangements for a party in the evening, and also work from home for an MNC. But all at once? NO, no, no. One by one? A big YES.

So let us be clear that we are human beings and not supermen or women. And the moment you try to be one, you are bound to feel overwhelmed, exhausted, irritated, and finally, IMPATIENT.

And we all have a capacity cap. This means we can do this much and only this much, period. Nature has fixed certain limits too. For example, the temperature cannot go below -273 degrees Celsius, known as absolute zero, or you cannot run 100 meters in eight seconds. Nothing can travel faster than the speed of light. So one must understand one's own limitations.

Whatever we plan therefore has to be realistic, practical, and workable. Hence, two things are very important: first, your plan must be workable, and second, it has to be simple—the simpler the better. KISS—Keep It Simple Stupid—is an often-used term, and I too would like to use it to keep things simple.

> Sometimes I think there are only two instructions we need to follow to develop and deepen our spiritual life: slow down and let go.
>
> —Oriah Mountain Dreamer

Prioritize Your Work Template

I would suggest that you do what I used to do when in high-pressure jobs. I still do the same, even as a full-time professional author today where I can work at my own pace—because habits die hard. Mind you, your work style has to become a habit, else it is no good.

I always use the good old dairy and pen/pencil to plan my day, which I do a day in advance, and as I get new inputs, I add them to my to-do list. I don't go for fancy electronic notebooks or expensive phones with organizers. I think I can do without them, and I have done very well with this method for several decades juggling between jobs. The problem I have with these devices is that when I get an idea/task in mind, I need to jot it down right then. Unfortunately, by the time the device gets ready, I usually forget the point. A diary and a pen is faster—even a napkin in a restaurant or a piece of toilet paper can work, but it has to be fast enough so it works. After jotting it down ASAP, I note it down in my office diary. I prefer simple, ruled diaries without dates as I put my own date.

Once I have a list of, say, fifteen tasks on a page of my diary, I mark the date on top and then see which the most urgent/important tasks are. It is not easy to set priorities, and this is the most difficult part. Here, it is your judgment that counts. I mark the top priority ones as P1, next P2, and third P3. People suggest five priorities—A, B, C, D, and E—but if you do not understand your work, you need to make five priorities, but if you do, you can manage it in three. Knowing your priorities moves you from being reactive to proactive. My prioritization works on the first-things-first principle.

The late Lee Iacocca said in one of his books, "If a CEO cannot make his turnaround plan for a sick company he takes over in one page—yes, one page—then he needs to be fired!" I totally agree with him. If your plan runs into twenty pages you don't know what the hell you are doing!

So yet again, folks, keep it simple. And that will work. There is no point in getting overwhelmed with the task that you are doing.

Balance Brought Forward

Once my day begins, I start with the P1 types one by one and keep scoring off or actually striking off once a job is done. At the end of the day my entire page looks messy, but my endeavor is achieved, and all my points, i.e., P1, P2, and P3 have been stricken off. Phew! And that is the ultimate high one gets. But this does not happen every day. Most days, you have a few points that have not been taken care off. I circle these and say, "I will sort you out tomorrow." Very patiently, I bring forward these points on to the next day's page. If I have three points that I carry forward, it means I finished a dozen today. This gives you a sense of achievement and the messy page is a great morale booster! I look at what is done and don't worry about what has not been finished. I need to tell my boss I give an interim report that these three jobs will be done tomorrow first thing in the morning and give reasons as to why these could not be done. SIMPLE. And let me tell you, it works so well that everyone is happy. You also delegate these tasks or associated work to your team and move on patiently.

All in a Day's Work

Learn to be "tactically selfish" at work and learn to say no and don't try to please everyone. This way you will be displeased with yourself and become unproductive, frustrated, and impatient with yourself.

While you are ticking off points efficiently, you will hit some speed breakers which pop up as urgent. These seemingly urgent require-ments are usually triggered by outside factors, like colleagues, sub-ordinates, or others. You need to keep your focus on the straight line that you have for the day. For you, it is those fifteen points, including P1 to P3, that is your focus and Key Result Areas (KRA). Never let your day get derailed by outside booby traps or bumpers. Only then will you work patiently and productively. Remember, it is not possible to stop these interruptions but it is always possible for you not to get interrupted by these interruptions.

The best way to be more productive is to be in your job fully. When you are working on something, it must have your hundred percent in it. No shortcuts, no distractions, no compromises. Give your best shot every time.

The best way to avoid getting overwhelmed by your to-do list is to focus your entire energy on the task at hand.

—Nico Prins

Delegate and Utilize the System

Organizations are created on purpose and the roles and responsibilities are very well defined. Don't underutilize the organization. For instance, if you have to travel for company work, let the admin department do your travel and stay arrangements for you. A mail, a note, or a brief chat on the intercom should do; don't try to be smart by doing it yourself, though you may be good at it. Taking someone else's work is not smartness, it is foolishness. Everyone is paid for his job, so are you. So do your job and let others do theirs.

Chewing the Cud

The Japanese are known to spend more time in planning meticulously so that execution becomes smoother and quicker. Exact percentages may not be available and may vary from project to project, but it is important to do due diligence, look at all the options, write out a full execution plan, place the teams in place, brief up to the last man, and then start rolling out your action. If all your supplies logistics, and people are ready, you will have no on-the-job hiccups at all and everything will go as planned. There is less frustration and no impatience as everything works with clockwork precision.

I follow a technique which I call "chewing the cud." This works very well when I write a book. Once I get an idea, I keep thinking about it almost 24/7. I sleep with the idea, I walk with it, I eat with it, and sometimes the idea becomes an obsession. I think deeply but in a random way about it, and some major parts of the plot/content start getting created. This takes a lot of time, and I don't put my pen to paper unless chewing the cud is completed and I am ready to go. In certain jobs, this can work very well, especially if you are in a creative field. I think patiently, without deadlines, and I enjoy every moment of chewing the cud. It is, in a way, a stress buster for me.

There is no One-Size-Fits-All Solution to Working Patiently

If you are better organized, you will be more efficient, less frustrated, more satisfied, and be more patient as there will be no room for impatience in such a style of working. So find out what works best for you and make this a habit—get organized, prioritize, and go for it.

Eating Food to Fully Enjoy it Patiently

There is a phrase in Hindi: *"Kaam karte ho to peit ki khatir,"* which means you work to fill up your stomach and have food on the table. This is the basic need of a human being.

But do we eat food patiently? Most of us don't. I am surprised when some people say. "I got so busy with work that I had my lunch at five in the evening and I had no time to have my breakfast." You must be mad—then what are you working for? Acidity, ulcers, or a heart attack. You might as well stop working. You are running on your life line too fast!

When you have your meal, you should be fully into it. In Indian culture, we eat with our hands, which is the touch. You look at the beauty of the food that you are eating, the way it is organized, then you smell the aroma, and finally, you put it in your mouth and taste it. Four of your senses get fully involved—sight, touch, smell, and taste.

This is maximum bang for the buck. No one should disturb you. Put your phone on silent and You concentrate only on the food and enjoy.

When You fall, Fall Like a Leaf
In life, if you ever fall, fall gracefully. Fall like a leaf falls from the tree—dancing gracefully.

> If there's one thing that I've repeatedly and rather foolishly forgotten to schedule into my life it is to create times where it's not scheduled.

—Craig D. Lounsbrough

7

Being in The Moment

*Many people are alive but don't touch the miracle of
being alive.*

—Thích Nhất Hạnh

WE EITHER LIVE in the past or the future, and that is one reason
for our dissatisfaction and being impatient.

Impatience is more to do with the future because all along a
soundtrack or a "future thought track" is playing in our heads, which
runs something like "let us preserve this for tomorrow, that for day
after, what will happen tomorrow, if this happens tomorrow, if that
happens."

A Live Concert I Attended

In 2015, Liz Mitchell, the lead singer of Boney M, who was at that time
sixty-three years old, was performing live in Pune, India, and I happened to attend the concert—a once-in-a-lifetime chance as I am a
huge fan of Boney M songs. To see her and watch her perform right
in front of me on the stage was like a dream come true.

She was so graceful, so full of energy, and she had the same brilliantly mesmerizing voice and same panache, and the audience went berserk. The venue was jam-packed, and the music was blasting from Bose speakers. The lady appeared in a shimmering black dress almost an hour after some junior artists played Boney M songs to hold the audience's attention. There were screams and whistles, and a rousing welcome was given to her.

As she started singing, to my surprise, almost every one took out their cell phones and started taking videos of the live performance. *How stupid of them*, I thought. *Here she is performing live, and you are taking a video!* OMG.

After her first song, she waved at the crowd, which was still busy shooting, and said, "Hey, look at me. All my videos are available on YouTube. You can watch them there again, all my songs. So now watch me."

Yet the crowd was so stupid that they continued taking videos for the rest of the performance. Each had spent a hefty amount to buy tickets. It is like buying a movie ticket and instead of watching the big screen, you start shooting the whole two-hour movie on your mobile camera.

I have attended meditation courses or Vipassana, which **teaches only** one thing—the power of now and to be in the present. Both my time and money would have been wasted in weeklong meditation camps as well as this concert if I had not learnt the lesson of being in the moment.

The same thing happens when you go on a holiday, either abroad or within the country. People are busy taking pictures and don't enjoy the moment. You are at the Leaning Tower of Pisa and you are not looking at the monument but clicking pictures all the time. Today, it has become worse because there is almost no cost attached to a picture on a phone camera. There is no processing cost and no cost for the film.

The best part is that after you come back from the holiday, you rarely look at the photos again—hundreds of them. You can see all these places on Nat Geo or the Discovery channel too. Then why did you spend so much on air travel and stay?

Fear of Missing Out
Today, most people suffer from the fear of missing out—the FOMO syndrome—and don't want to miss out on anything. We are touch-and-go TOGO visitors who want to tick the box. "Oh I saw fifty places in Rome." Fifty places? You must be crazy! You probably spent a few minutes at each location, running from one to another. Had you visited only three or five, you would have absorbed more, and yet you were impatient to run from one to the other like crazy. This is like incessantly clicking pictures—both types waste money.

> Quiet the mind, and the soul will speak.

> —Ma Jaya Sati Bhagavati

Meditation: Stillness of Mind
Every meditation method tries to teach one basic thing—how to keep your mind calm.

I attended a ten-day course on Vipassana, which is a meditation technique developed by Gautama Buddha almost two thousand six hundred years ago, and the whole aim of that ten-day effort was to learn to be calm, to make your mind absolutely stationary.

> It is better to conquer yourself than to win a thousand battles. Then the victory is yours. It cannot be taken from you.

> —Buddha

The technique is very simple but not easy to perform. The idea is to tame our mind, which is agitated all the time. Our mind is always thinking of the past or the future—it is never in the now, the present moment. It is like a wild elephant, and if you tie it to a pillar with a chain, it make all efforts to free itself; it screams, yells for days on, and after a few days, it dawns on him that this screaming and yelling will not help, and he calms down. Similarly, our mind is always screaming and yelling as something is always troubling us. We need to nail it down to a virtual pillar so that, after sometime, it becomes calm like the proverbial elephant. Yes, our mind is always agitated, and meditation is a way to calm it down. This agitation is the cause of frustration, restlessness, and impatience.

Learn this from water: loud splashes the brook but the oceans depth are calm.

—Buddha

Vipassana Explained

Vipassana teaches us how to stop getting impatient.Mere reading won't help—you need to learn it under an *acharya* or guru/ teacher, and then keep practicing it later to reap its benefits. But it works wonders.

The meditator sits in a quiet place and concentrates on his breathing. You watch your breathing as it moves out of the nostrils and moves into the nostrils. It can be shallow, deep, hot, cool, or cold; you just observe and don't react. Watch, don't react. Watch, don't react. As your mind wanders—which it does—you bring it back again to your breathing. After a few days, it stops wandering or wanders much less, and calm prevails.

The next step, which is after a few days, is that you observe feeling in your body, right from head to toes, inch by inch. You feel sensations of different types, sometimes, hard, soft, heat, cold, or feeling irritation on the skin, sometimes a dead zone, sometimes a superactive zone, pain, or no pain at all, stiffness, a relaxed feeling on the surface, etc. Again watch these sensations without prejudice, malice, hatred, or happiness—just watch the sensation and don't react and move on. Sounds simple? Try it. You will discover that your mind is never in your control and wanders very quickly. You have to bring it back on track and keep doing it till you master this technique.

Therefore, to be patient, one can learn any meditation technique. I have briefly described what I have learnt. It definitely helps.

Try to enjoy the moment rather than taking selfies or videos of something that you have made an effort to see.

> The best way to capture moments is to pay attention. This is how we cultivate mindfulness.
>
> —Jon Kabat-Zinn

8

How to use Social Media and the Mobile Phone to Build Patience

Patience isn't something that gets handed out to some and not to others. It is a skill you can develop through understanding and practice.

HOW DO WE? use social media, using our cell phone and computer, to build patience? Sounds weird? I will explain how it is possible.

Frustration is a feeling of agitation and helplessness triggered when your needs are not met. Life is not a bed of roses, you will never get everything that you want, and there will be some achievements and some failures. We have become too used to immediate results. E-mails zip across the globe in seconds. You can get the temperature of any city at the click of your mouse. If a picture doesn't download immediately, you fret and fume and yell as if the heavens have fallen.

Frustration is an emotion that makes us tense, kills our sense of humor, and sometimes makes our life miserable. This can lead to serious problems like sadness, depression, and even suicide. Conquering frustration will revive your emotional life by making it your choice as to how you handle daily hassles and stress .You have a choice—either remain frustrated at your own peril or transform yourself with the greatest virtue, patience.

> Patience is not simply the ability to wait—it's how we behave while we're waiting.
>
> —Joyce Meyer

Social media as an all important tool which can be cleverly used for our benefit in more than one way.

All of us use social media for several hours every day. WhatsApp, Facebook, Instagram, and Twitter—this is the usual order of preference in most cases. So much so that unfortunately, these tools which are supposed to connect us to the rest of the world, especially our near and dear ones, have become big time wasters, and most of us are almost addicted to them. Since all these are available on mobile phones, they can be accessed 24/7, even while walking on the road, sitting in a park, having a discussion with a friend, watching TV, or traveling in a train or a bus. We feel that without this our life will become very difficult, or worse, meaningless. Next time you go to an airport or a waiting room in a railway station, just count how many people are sitting busy with their phones. I bet you will smile—almost 90 percent of them will be on their laptops or phones as if sky is going to fall.In fact, today, a mobile is our most prized possession, which we don't let go off even for a minute.If you can let go of your mobile, you can acquire patience.

Watch your mobile but don't react to its beeps, vibrations, and ringing. That can be electronic meditation. Use it as electronic Vipassana, which we discussed in the last chapter.

You can do the following to build patience by using your mobile wisely.

1. *Decide on daily mobile-free hours*: We have sixteen waking hours in a day. Decide on disciplined use by allotting two-hour windows where you will keep your phone on silent mode. Three such windows can reduce usage by six hours. The heavens won't fall if you don't respond to calls. You should check for missed call alerts and respond selectively thereafter. Once you get used to this, make four windows. This way, you will build self-control, discipline, and restraint.
2. *Never use your mobile after 10:00 p.m.*: This can be easily done if you have the willpower or you want to develop willpower. After all, willpower is nothing but having a will and the power to execute that will.
3. *Have patience*: Don't respond to every message or tweet or a post on Facebook. Apply three filters before you respond. Is this information useful, is it true, and is this good information? Otherwise delete.
4. *Have the power to delete*: Have the courage to delete a mail or a message that is useless. This makes you more resolute and determined.
5. *Be brief*: This is important. Don't keep chatting for nothing. Have the willpower to hang up and say bye to the person you are speaking to. Be polite but firm and diplomatic.
6. *Kill the forwarding itch*: This is the most difficult thing to do. We all do this every day; we forward most messages on WhatsApp to all and sundry. If you can stop this, you have achieved almost a ten on ten in willpower.
7. *Avoid joining groups*: These are the biggest time wasters. Unless it helps you learn something, quit the useless ones.
8. *Mobile fasting*: People fast on some days of the week, where they do not eat food. This is to give rest to your system and also build self-control through self-denial. Try to do this with

your mobile. Switch it off or keep it on silent mode for the whole day. Can you do this once a week? If you can, you have built the strongest willpower and determination in your character. You will then develop tremendous self-control.

9. *Forget it on purpose:* When you go out for a walk or to a friend's house or to play with friends, don't carry your mobile with you. Inform your parents too. Nothing will happen if you don't have it with you. You need to get used to not using it; build a habit of depriving yourself of the phone on purpose. This again builds willpower.

10. *Don't worry about likes:* Sometimes we post on Facebook and expect people to like our post or comment positively. This is not necessary. Don't worry about the number of likes. The world won't end if some people don't like your ideas. This builds resilience and patience.

11. *Don't react to obnoxious messages that are meant to incite you:* Read and watch but don't react. Gautama Buddha's biggest teaching is: "Watch don't react." This is a two-pronged approach to build character. First, it gives you peace of mind, and second, it builds strong character and patience.

12. *Put a sticker on your mobile:* Write "Keep me away for a while please. I am your mobile but I also get tired," and add an angry emoji. You could do this on your laptop too. If you listen to your own message, you have become master of yourself and master of self-control.

13. *Control the morning itch:* Most of us start looking for our mobile phone the moment we get up. Develop self-control by saying a firm no to yourself and read the newspaper or listen to the radio, but do not pick up the phone before you have had breakfast or at a time you fix for yourself.

14. *Move away from the laptop as much as possible:* If you have a laptop, don't remain glued to it the whole day. Go for a walk, play some outdoor games, or read a book or magazine.

15. *Don't watch movies or clips on the mobile*: Do not watch movies or short videos on the mobile. Get rid of this habit; by doing this you develop self-restraint

16. *Inform friends of your decision*: Have the courage to inform your friends that you have made certain resolutions to build your willpower and patience and that they should understand and appreciate your resolve

17. *Make it your style statement*: "No to plastic, no to substance abuse, and no to mobiles." Start a campaign in your friends' circle and ask people to share this message. Remember, this message is useful, good, and truthful. It passes the test of three filters. Be a leader all the way. You will earn respect.

18. *Create positive peer pressure on others*: You make your own rules and you are the best. Remember Amitabh Bachchan's dialogue: *"Line wahan say shuru hoti hai jahan hum khadey hotey hain."* (Line starts from where I stand) You need to take a call, and for that you require guts, determination, and patience. Remember, without guts there is no glory. Instead of coming under negative peer pressure, you create peer pressure on others by using social media and the mobile for your own good.

19. *Try this*: Don't text messages while walking on the road and no phone calls while driving.

20. *Never annoy others with your behavior*: Never text or speak to any one while at the dining table or having tea or snacks with friends. You need to have self-control to do this.

21. *It's now in your hands*: Remember the tool, i.e., the mobile, to develop willpower and patience is right in your hands. This tool allows you to become stronger in character and in any which way you look at yourself. Remember great people are still great who don't use a mobile. Did you know that Tom Cruise, Sarah Jessica Parker, and even Warren Buffet don't use a mobile at all? If they can, so can you.

You Can't Do it Alone

We live with friends and relatives who also use the phone very erratically. They too are struggling with how to keep themselves away from this addiction to the phone and social media. Were people not living well and were they not happy when mobiles were not invented? Yes, they were. People from those days will tell you that they had a much more relaxed life and more free time those days.

Since everyone is using mobiles and social media, you have to take people along with you. Else people will misunderstand you and may label you as a recluse. It is therefore better to tell your close friends and relatives whom you communicate very frequently about your resolve and why you are doing it. Yes you tell them that you are taking this action to build your will power, patience and self-control. Some may disagree but that is where your will must prevail. Tell them about your plans which you can make considering the points given above. Tell them the time you will not use the phone, your mobile fast day and windows of absence. You have to be a leader with strong will and resilience. Gradually people will understand and as you inspire them they may follow your footsteps. In fact it will be better to make a closed user group of say ten friends and some relatives to take this mission forward. You can involve your parents too;more the better.

If you want this mission impossible to be mission possible you got to use your art of persuasion to convince others. This is a bonus too. When you have a big enough group you will find that your ambition and mission is accomplished. If you are able to do all this keeping will power, patience and self-control then you will be a winner and you will see how positive and how strong you have become. You may have withdrawal symptoms like a detoxification effect but you have to have a strong will to carry on regardless and to achieve your goal come what may.

It is Electronic Mental floss.

Don't bite more than you can chew

We have seen twenty one ways of using social media and mobile phones to build will power and patience. You need not start with all of them together. Take up three to five suggestions and implement them to the full extent. This way your plan and effort will be successful. Taking too much on your plate may discourage you and cause frustration. It is better to go step by step. Let me assure you this - that in the long run your efforts will transform your personality and change your life to become a better person and will help you succeed in whatever you plan to do in the future.

"Great works are performed not by strength but by perseverance."

—Samuel Johnson

9
On Doing Nothing

Don't underestimate the value of "Doing Nothing," of just going along, listening to all the things you can't hear, and not bothering.

—AA Milne

I LOVE THIS. I read this essay—on doing nothing—by JB Priestley, or part of it, when I was in school, and believe me, it still resonates many, many decades after. It makes such profound sense. It is a perfect recipe for detox and mental floss.

Two friends walk up a mountain trail and go up a flat top, lie flat on their backs, and look into the sky, into the oblivion, looking nowhere. With its velvety patches, no bigger than a drawing-room carpet, of fine moorland grass, its surfaces invite repose. Birds and eagles fly, free-flying objects making full use of thermals without flapping wings, just gliding away, is a kind of clean bare antechamber to heaven. The early afternoon sky is clear, and one can see some clouds floating like balls of cotton; they split and merge into different shapes, sometimes you see a tiger, sometimes an elephant, and in minutes an old woman. It is so relaxing, on doing nothing. This is so good for mental health when you let go of your past and do not worry about the future. They did eat sandwiches and a cold drink/water which they carried with them, never bothered about what the rest of the world was doing in the town below.

I remember going for such picnics with friends in those good old days, and one is reminded of the song "Koi Lauta De Mere Beetey Hue Din" (can someone get me those golden days back?). Some people would call it a criminal waste of time, a waste of life. Well, I feel doing this once in a while—an unplanned visit to a jungle nearby, a garden, or a mountaintop and lying down and lazing around with an absolute blank mind can do us wonders. The problem today is that even for pleasure, we plan. A picnic is organized chaos—you carry loads of packed food, a music system, chairs, tables . . . What the hell! Is it a punishment? And then, in the evening, you wind up, pack up, and go home—tired from the noise of people yelling at each other and the blaring music. You went for that? No, you must go only to do nothing.

One could do this at night, and we did it during the good old days. Lying flat on the *charpoy*, looking into the crystal-clear sky, identifying the Milky Way, Pole Star, and Pleiades, also known as the Seven Sisters. Pleiades is actually an open star cluster located in the constellation of Taurus. If we were lucky, we would see a shooting star with its bright tail. The experience was electrifying yet soothing.

Today we live in urban areas where these luxuries are not available, and gurus suggest that we start the day with quiet time, sitting in the corner of a room and thinking nothing, keeping your mind blank—doing nothing.

To do anything, it is first necessary to be doing nothing.

—Nancy Hale

Laziness is the Worst Sin

"How is laziness or doing nothing connected to being patient?" you may ask. Try to do nothing. Doing nothing itself requires a lot of patience because most of us are so fidgety, frisky, and restless that you often hear people saying, "Oh, man, how can you stay at home for so many hours? I get very restless without work." Such people are restlessly impatient. Being lazy can save the world as well.

Had people not been overenthusiastic and overenergetic, the world would have been saved/spared from the destruction, deaths, and misery of the two great world wars. And we still call them great, whereas there was nothing great about them.

Let me quote a few paragraphs from the essay written by JB Priestley to reveal his point of view about these wars. You need to know a little more about the history of these wars to appreciate this better.

All the evil in this world brought by persons who are always up and doing, but do not know when they ought to be up nor what they ought to be doing. The devil, I take it, is still the busiest creature in the universe, and I can quite imagine him denouncing laziness and becoming angry at the smallest waste of time. In his kingdom (Devil's), I will wager, nobody is allowed to do nothing, not even for a single afternoon.

The world, we all freely admit, is in a muddle, but I for one do not think that it is laziness that brought it to such a pass. It is not the active virtue that it lacks but passive ones; it is capable of anything but kindness and a little steady thought. There is still plenty of energy in the world (there never were more fussy people about), but most of it is simply misdirected. If, for example, in July 1914, when there was some capital idling weather, everybody, emperor, kings, archdukes, statesmen, generals, journalists, had been suddenly smitten with an intense desire to do nothing, just to hang around in the sunshine and consume tobacco, then we should all have been much better off than we are now. But no, then we should all have been much better off than we are now. But no, the doctrine of the strenuous life still went unchallenged; there must be no time wasted; something must be done. And, as we know, something was done. World War I had begun.

Again, after the defeat of Germany in 1919 after WWI was over, suppose our statesmen, instead of rushing off to Versailles with a bundle of ill-digested notions and a great deal of energy to dissipate, had all taken a fortnight off, away from all correspondence and interviews and what not, and had simply lounged about on some hillside or other, apparently doing nothing for the first time in their energetic lives, then they might have gone to their so called Peace Conference and come away again with their reputations still unsoiled and the affairs of the world in good trim.

Even at the present time, if half the politicians in Europe would relinquish the notion that laziness is a crime and go away and do nothing for a little space, we should certainly gain by it. Other examples come crowding into the mind. Thus, every now and then, certain religious sects hold conferences; but though there are evils abroad that are mountains high, though the fate of civilization is still doubtful, the members who attend these conferences spend their time condemning the length of ladies' skirts and the noisiness of dance bands. They would all be better employed lying flat on their backs somewhere, staring at the sky and recovering their mental health.

To Do Nothing is the Most Difficult Thing to Do

People keep saying today, "Oh, life is so boring."

I remember when I was once posted to Shimla. It was a pleasant ritual to stroll on the Mall Road—from Cecil Hotel at one end to the Clarks at the other. People would just stroll casually and chat about whatever came to their mind; there was no hurry, just a lazy walk— no brisk walking please. It was an exercise for the soul and not for the body as such—body exercise was just incidental, a bonus. People had umbrellas in hand, and if it drizzled, all the umbrellas unfolded and it was like a scene from a film with thousands of them flipping open together. There was still no rush. Everyone enjoyed the drizzle.

Children, young, and the old, every one strolled—doing nothing. May be one would stop to pick up a chicken patty or a coffee or popcorn on the way from tuck shops. Everything smelled better on that stroll— better than the rush hour in metros.

There were four guests from Bombay (now Mumbai) at my neighbor's house. They had come to a hill station for the first time. Very enthusiastically, my friend took them to the Mall, which was something every visitor would be taken to, as if it was a visit to a holy place—yes, a ritual no guest should miss. They started walking, and after five minutes they realized that the crowd just didn't move! It moved, but not at the speed at which Bombay moves. In metros like Bombay, people run to catch a train, jump off a BEST bus, run and hail a cab, and run fast not to miss the lift to take them to the twentieth floor. Run, run, and run. So unfortunate, isn't it? They had a problem with doing nothing! The eldest guest said, "*Yaar*, it is damn boring, no one moves here. How do they manage?" They were told to just chill, but they were so restless that they went back to Bombay in five days flat, cutting short their vacation. It was not possible for them to do nothing!

Today, the younger generation comes up with fancy terms: emptiness within, boring life, no adrenalin, no challenge, no action, I wanna be where the action is.

Whenever something seems boring, it means we have no patience for it. You can't sit in a place for five minutes for the waiter to serve you tomato soup. You want it the best, the hottest, and you want it right now. It is boring to wait; actually, you are impatient. That is why microwaves came. You want a refrigerator to make ice in ten minutes, a rice cooker to do it fast, a curd maker, and the darn list goes on and on.

The COVID-19 pandemic has brought some sense of ease into our lives. We were forced to stay at home doing nothing. Imagine the world is locked up for a good twenty months—no schools, no offices, no eating out, no cinema, no picnics—yet we survived. We relaxed and got closer to our families.

During childhood, we saw a sense of participation. We had an ice-cream maker which was a hand-cranked machine. You had to fill ice pieces around the metal drum and also some salt to lower the temperature. The whole family used to take part in this exercise, which made you wait for hours to get a scoop of ice-cream. It depends on you, whether you take it as a fun game or punishment. It is how you look at it.

Today you want an ice-cream in a minute from a shop.

10

Handling Rage

Be Patient with Your Anger

Anyone can become angry—that is easy.
But to be angry with the right person, to the right
degree, at the right time, for the right purpose,
and in the right way, is not easy.

—Aristotle

The Devil in Us

Rage is uncontrollable anger where you lose control of your actions—you may swear, abuse, and even hit out at someone. One witnesses such scenes on the road, you read about it in newspapers, or see disturbing visuals on TV. This is caused by our mental state and the environment around us.

You can do little to change the environment—in fact, you can do nothing to change it. If there is traffic on the road, you cannot change it; if there is a learner driving in front of you, it is not possible to change the situation. If he is in front of you, he is in front; you can do nothing about it. Honking, gesturing, and shouting will make him more nervous, and he may have an accident, for which you will be blamed. If there is a traffic jam because of an accident or a truck getting overturned on the highway, again, you can't do anything. These are situations caused by external factors over which you have little or no control.

Yet rage and anger get the better of us almost on a daily basis. Actually, the devil of impatience is within us. What you can control is your reaction to the situation.

The Importance of Our Emotions

Displaying emotions is a manageable art. You cannot appear to be thick-skinned and have no feelings at all. Display of positive as well as negative emotional responses to situations is very important for our relationships with people. Display of positive emotions can earn goodwill. It has a soothing effect on our friends and family.

At the same time, appropriate displays of negative emotional responses like anger, displeasure, anxiety, and criticism are also a part of our emotional repository and a part of our being. These are demonstrated by every human being in some measure under different circumstances. But, oversensitivity and lack of self-control both spell doom—they invoke responses disproportionate to situations.

People respect those who are calm and composed even in a crisis. Novelist Ernest Hemingway very aptly said, "Courage is grace under pressure." It is therefore very important to have control of our feelings. Let us control our feelings before they control us!

Controlling Emotional Turbulence

The deadly emotional external tripwire

We have no control on when an emotion will be triggered. We also have little control on the form that the emotion will eventually take. This can be attributed simply to the fact that our emotions are generated as a response to a situation, and the reference point is external, over which we have no control. Each situation acts like a tripwire, invoking a reflex action from our side. There are simple common sense-based methods that can help us once we hit the tripwire.

> We cannot avoid birds from flying overhead but we can always stop them from making a nest in our hair.
>
> —Chinese proverb

The Dwell Time
We have no control on unforeseen situations that generate emotions, for instance, witnessing an accident or someone abusing a close friend, but we do have control to some extent on how long that emotion is going to last. This is what I would phrase as the "dwell time." Dwell means to live in a place, like a home is known as a dwelling unit. Let that emotion—if it is a negative one—not make a permanent home in your head. Shake it off as early as possible—and this can be done, because it is in your hands. You can at least make a sincere effort towards it. If somebody says something unpleasant, you can feel bad, but don't sulk and make your own life miserable. The art of handling yourself and living well is to reduce the dwell time of negative emotions.

There is an old saying in Hindi, which is a curse: *"Main tujhe saat janam tak maaf nahin karoonga,"* (I will not forgive you for next seven generations). In fact, by saying this, you are not cursing the other person, you are cursing yourself! You will keep that in mind for seven generations and keep sulking for that long? You have to be crazy to do so.

Use your rational mind to control your emotional mind
Nature has given us human beings a rational mind; use it to control the emotional mind when you hit an external tripwire. When animals

react to external inputs, they seldom know where to stop. That is why we use the expression "barking like a dog" for someone who blabbers unendingly. If a door without a latch bangs whenever there is a breeze, a dog will bark every time that it bangs, no matter how many times it happens during the night. However, we will handle it differently. We humans would examine the door once, and on noticing that there is no latch, would make a mental note of the fact that there is no latch and thereafter stop reaching out every time the door bangs. The very next day, we would take action to get the door repaired. Convincing yourself out of a situation or reconciling to a reality is the key to controlling emotional turbulence.

Patience is an antidote to anger and rage. If you are stuck in a traffic jam, you have several options on how to act. First, you can curse the municipality, your town management, the government, and even the chief minister. Second, you can get out of the car and walk ahead to see what has happened, and in the bargain, hurl out abuses left, right, and center, just throwing up your hands every time you abuse. This will not change the situation. Third, you get into the car and keep honking. Nothing will still matter or change. The fourth option is to open your laptop and make a PPT your boss wants in the evening, put on some music, and relax. These are all practical options, and you need to just make a choice. This is the test of patience we are put under almost every day. How can you afford to yell daily when there will be umpteen such occasions every day?

Let not the sun go down upon your wrath.

—The Bible

11
Some Exercises

Let Us Do It

Nature does not hurry, yet everything is accomplished.

—Lao Tzu

Fast Sickness

Fast sickness has hit us fast. Today we suffer from hurry-itus. Because of this, we lose out on the basic pleasures of life. Remember, *"Zindagi na milegi dobara,"* (you won't get a second chance in life). This whole book is about the virus of "fast sickness," and now we need to practice because practice makes a man perfect.

> Most men pursue pleasure with such breathless haste that they hurry past it.
>
> *—Søren Kierkegaard*

We don't have to create fancy exercises as we already have enough on our plate—we need to use daily scenarios to work on our patience quotient.

Sample these:
We have phrases like: "hit the ground running" or "speed is God" or "think at the speed of light" or "perform or perish" or "if you don't do it, somebody else will." These are all nutcrackers as they crack your head and coax you to push yourself.

Instead, we need signboards today that read like "relax and chill" or "if you don't do it, someone else will do it for you" or "don't be fidgety," or "go slow; the heavens won't fall" or "take it easy" or "this is not the end of the world" or "mistakes will happen" (I had put this one in my office once). These are nut soothers.

Today doctors' visits are under nine minutes, dentists promise root canal treatments in two short sittings, elevators take you up in seconds across forty stories. We can't wait for our computer to boot for more than a minute, Disprin to dissolve in seconds, headaches to go in six minutes, Eno to give relief from gas in six seconds, our blocked nose to be cleared in twenty-three seconds, Vicks to work in thirty seconds, stomach to be cleared in two minutes. We can't rest in peace even on the pot. Damn it! The day has twenty-four hours, which is 86,400 seconds.

Metros take six minutes between stations. Hurry, hurry, and hurry, but where to?

I had a boss who always was in a hurry, and his favorite phrase was, "as of yesterday." So I made a joke in the office by taking an oath: *"Main jo bhi karoonga jaldi karoonga, jaldi ke siva kuch nahi karoonga,"* (Whatever I do, I will do quickly, and nothing but quickly) which is like an oath you take while deposing in front of a judge in the court: *"Main Gita ki kasam khaa kar kehta hoon main job hi kahoonga, such kahoonga, such ke ilawa kuch nahin kahoonga."* (I swear on the sacred *Gita* that whatever I say will be the truth and nothing but the truth)

You can take charge of your impatience bug by doing the following:

1. Today you have a no-horn day. We all press on the car or two-wheeler horn all the time. Stop it.

2. Control the electronic itch. We keep forwarding messages on WhatsApp. Use this as a tool to develop patience—look at it but don't forward.

3. Stop peeping into your phone every minute. Make a promise to yourself to check your phone every two hours only.

4. Once a week, do mobile fasting by leaving your phone at home. The heavens won't fall and you will have a great day. You need courage to do it; you can always apologize later if required.

5. You will not press the button of your lift more than once and will wait patiently and once the lift comes, don't jump in; wait for people to get out and then get in with ease.

6. Eat your food slowly—don't gulp it down.

7. While having your meals, keep your phone on silent and have a peaceful, hearty meal. You can, at the end of the meal, have a look at the missed calls/messages and respond peacefully. I do this, and it works wonders. We feel that the world will stop working if we take a few hours off. Forget it, no one is missing you. If you are in a chauffeur-driven car, read the newspaper or a book. Learn while you move.

8. At a crossing at the traffic signal, switch off the car/bike. In a car, listen to music and don't honk at the green light. On a two-wheeler, you can hum a song.

9. If you feel you are going to become impatient, try the old method of counting till ten, or if required, till twenty.

10. Standing in a line or queue, hum a song or think of your childhood or of a vacation. Keep your mind occupied. Here you could use your phone to send pending messages and use as well as kill the time.

11. Stop sulking and try to remain relaxed. Remember, it is a choice you make to remain cool.

Try these things on a daily basis and you will succeed. Keep saying to yourself, "Yes, I can," and you will see that you can.

If you have a problem that is bothering you, do the following things:

a. Write down the problem on a piece of paper—this helps you understand the problem better.
b. See what's the best that can be done under the circumstances.
c. Think about the worst-case scenario and what the consequences will be.
d. Accept the consequences (this relieves the pressure from your heart and mind).
e. Now try your best to solve the problem as per point b above.

This way you will be able to patiently solve the problem to the best of your ability and according to the circumstances.

Games can be very challenging and soothing too. Take the example of golf.

This is a game that is very technical, requires patience, and can be used to build patience. It depends on you.

I started this game quite late in life, and I was rightly advised by a friend to hire a coach, which I did. We went on to the driving range, and I was taught the basics and finally learnt how to take a swing and hit the ball. It requires a lot of patience for the first couple of months because nothing seems to work. The first few weeks are very frustrating, and one feels like quitting. But one has to do it every day for hours together, patiently trying to hit the small ball with a small club head. But once you get the hang of it, you will be in a hurry to go to the golf course and play the game. Here again, you require patience to hold on and continue for more time on the practice range. My coach was keen that I should get the feel of the golf course, but I refused. I wanted to spend more time learning before jumping onto the course. And this helped, as my game from day one became good and playable. The same applies to the greens. Putting is a game of patience. One must measure each shot and never be in a hurry to score.

Try your hand at fishing if you can. This also requires lot of patience.

It is easier to find men who will volunteer to die, than to find those who are willing to endure pain with patience.

—Julius Caesar

12
Love Yourself

Accept Things as They Are—Don't Try to Turn the World Around

Loving yourself isn't vanity. It's sanity.

—Andre Gide

YES, YOU HEARD it right: don't try to turn the world around, because if you try that, nothing will happen to the world, but you will get turned around and will get cramps in your brain!

The whole idea of patience is to be merciful to yourself, to have pity on yourself. The world will not change for you; you will have to change according to the world.

Don't try to be a perfectionist; don't try to achieve the unachievable and try to prove to the world that you are the best, you are the greatest. Get off that high horse. You get this life just once, don't let it get wasted. Get your foot off the gas pedal. Live life and don't make your own life miserable.

Life should be like tutti-frutti with chocolate sauce for your heart and not a drab vanilla scoop. Don't worry about how many candies or fruits it has; one less won't matter as long as the whole ice-cream is good. Put more chocolate sauce if you want. Play the game and don't keep counting the score. Have mercy on yourself; treat yourself with dignity and tender love . . . and enjoy. Sometimes forgive yourself—don't keep flogging yourself. Tomorrow may be too late. Yes, too late.

In this rat race, don't look for nuts only and miss out on the chunk of cheese lying on the side.

If you have lemons, make lemonade. Put some crushed ice and make it taste better. Make the best of what you have and what comes your way. Live life on daily basis: *kal ho na ho . . .* (If there is a tomorrow or not)

> Make your ego porous. Will is of little importance, complaining is nothing, fame is nothing. Openness, patience, receptivity, solitude is everything.

> —Rainer Maria Rilke

Self-Assessment Questions— Patience Shortgasm

1. What do you understand by patience and its importance in our lives?
2. Explain what patience on emotional as well as time continuum is?
3. Explain the quote "I have seen many storms in my life. Most storms have caught me by surprise, so I had to learn very quickly to look further and understand that I am not capable of controlling the weather, to exercise the art of patience and to respect the fury of nature."
4. Explain what you understand by "wishes are not always granted."
5. Give an example from your experience where your patience was put to test and you succeeded.
6. Explain in your own words "Nothing is permanent, neither happiness nor pain."
7. "We spend time on counting the score rather than playing the game." Explain this in your own words.

8. Explain what you understand by the following philosophical quote in your own words.

   "I can calculate everything but not the number of moments in a second."

                           —Khalid Masood

9. What is the best way to eat food and get the maximum out of it?
10. Why do numbers trouble us?
11. Explain your life as a line till now. What were important points you encountered on the line?
12. Multitasking is a myth as explained in the book. Explain with a personal example.
13. Explain what you understand by "Sometimes I think there are only two instructions we need to follow to develop and deepen our spiritual life: slow down and let go."
14. How do you prioritize your work after reading this book? Do you have any other way?
15. What do you understand by being in the moment? Explain in 200 words with an example.
16. "Doing nothing is the greatest thing to do." Explain its benefits in your own words.
17. Explain the quote in your own words. "Anyone can become angry—that is easy. But to be angry with the right person, to the right degree, at the right time, for the right purpose, and in the right way, is not easy."
18. What do you understand by "dwell time of rage?"
19. Give seven practical ways to control your impatience.
20. "Loving yourself isn't vanity. It's sanity." Explain in your own words with an example.